MY FIRST BODY MAP

ANATOMY FOR KIDS WORKBOOK

Children's Anatomy Books

BABY PROFESSOR
EDUCATION KIDS

Speedy Publishing LLC
40 E. Main St. #1156
Newark, DE 19711
www.speedypublishing.com

LET'S LEARN TOGETHER

BODY SYSTEMS

Here we will learn the different parts of the body as well as the body systems

CIRCULATORY SYSTEM

DIGESTIVE SYSTEM

MUSCULAR SYSTEM

NERVOUS SYSTEM

RESPIRATORY SYSTEM

SKELETAL SYSTEM

LEARN THE BODY PARTS WITH THE ALPHABET

arm

LEARN THE BODY PARTS WITH THE ALPHABET

LEARN THE BODY PARTS WITH THE ALPHABET

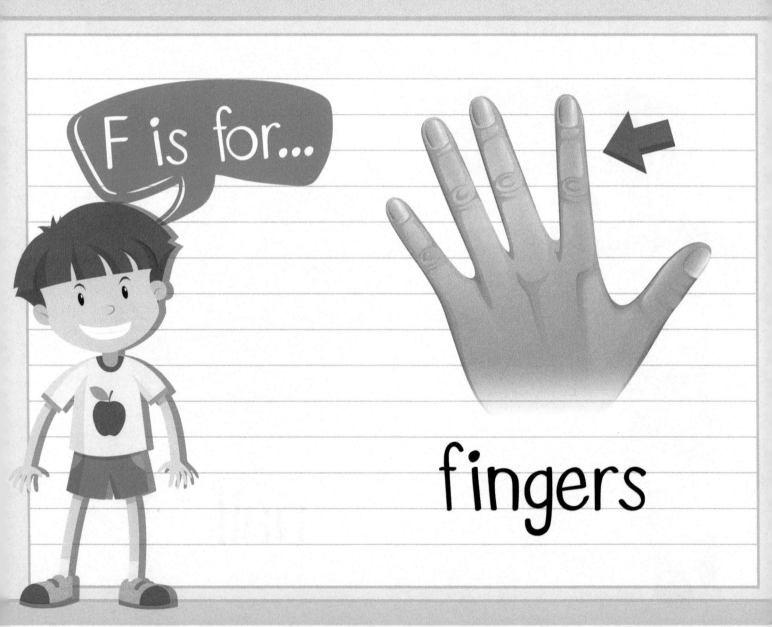

fingers

LEARN THE BODY PARTS WITH THE ALPHABET

LEARN THE BODY PARTS WITH THE ALPHABET

elbow

LEARN THE BODY PARTS WITH THE ALPHABET

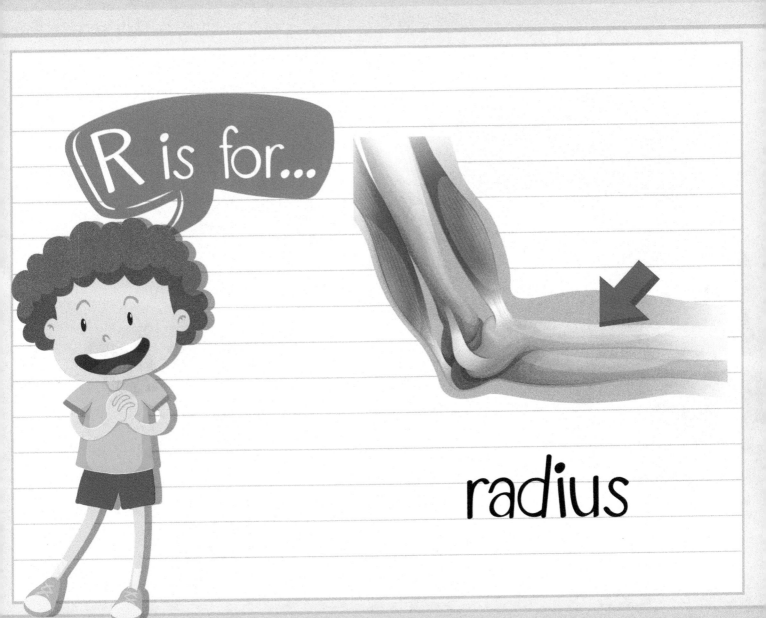

radius

LEARN THE BODY PARTS WITH THE ALPHABET

LEARN THE BODY PARTS WITH THE ALPHABET

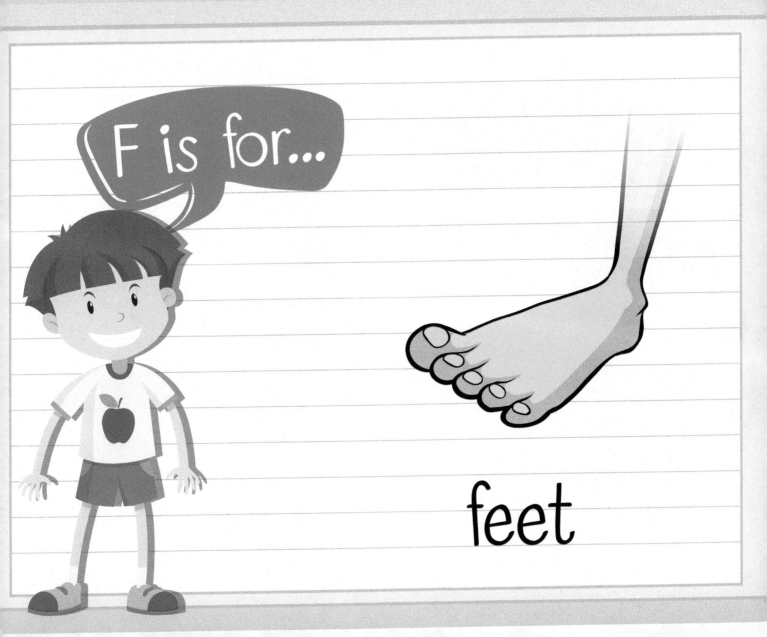

feet

LEARN THE BODY PARTS WITH THE ALPHABET

LEARN THE BODY PARTS WITH THE ALPHABET

A is for...

ankle

LEARN THE BODY PARTS WITH THE ALPHABET

LEARN THE BODY PARTS WITH THE ALPHABET

LEARN THE BODY PARTS WITH THE ALPHABET

LEARN THE BODY PARTS WITH THE ALPHABET

mouth

LEARN THE BODY PARTS WITH THE ALPHABET

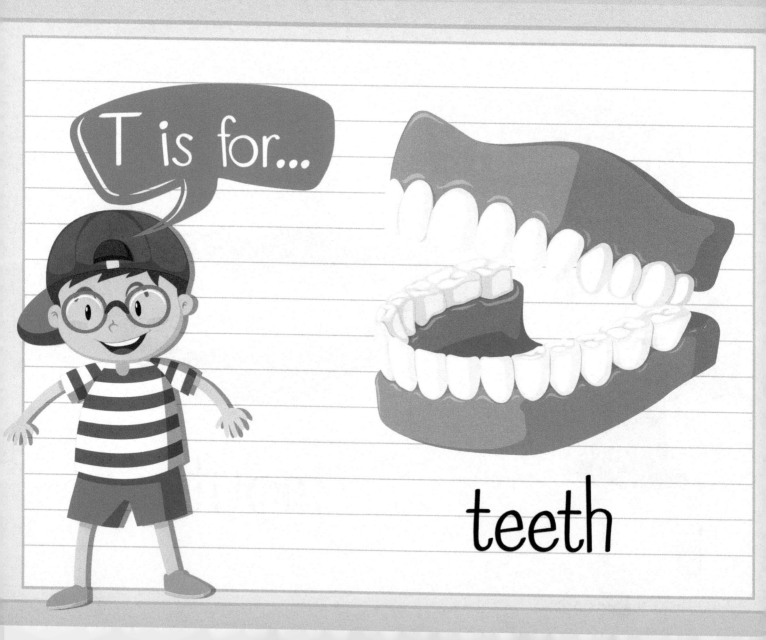

T is for...

teeth

LEARN THE BODY PARTS WITH THE ALPHABET

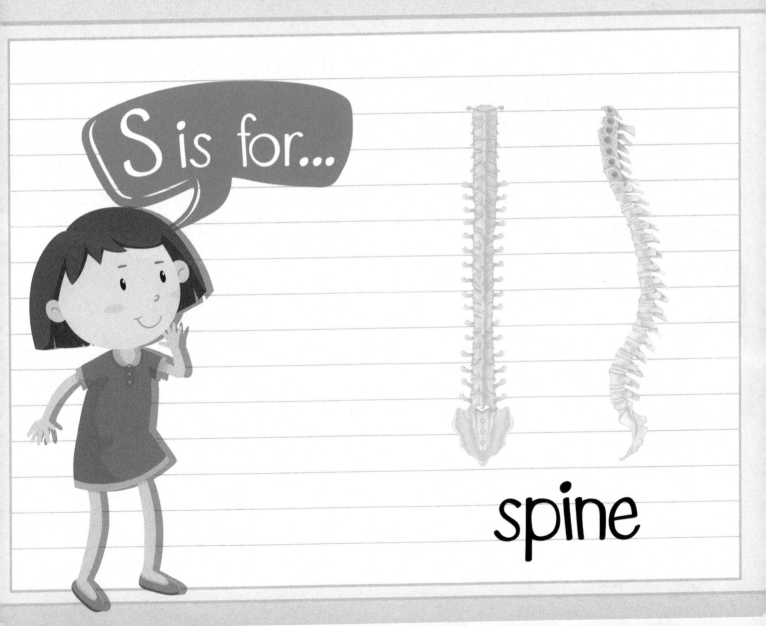

spine

LEARN THE BODY PARTS WITH THE ALPHABET

LEARN THE BODY PARTS WITH THE ALPHABET

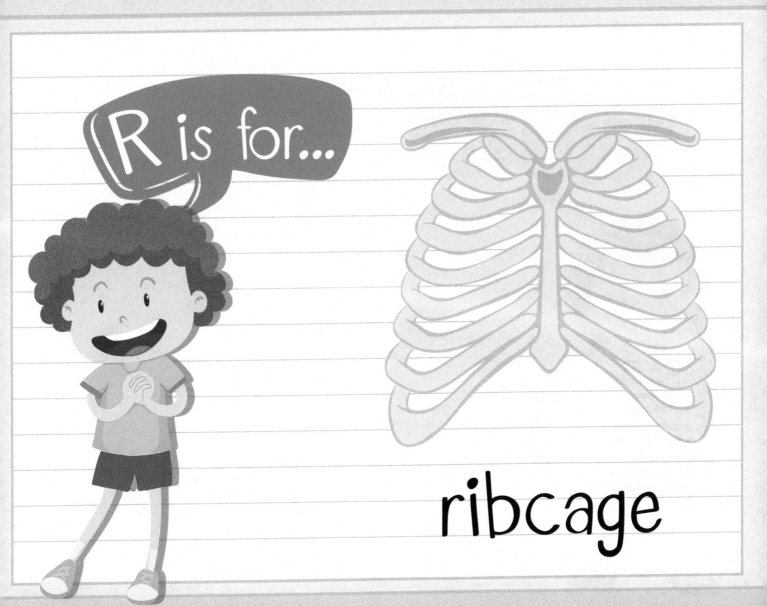

R is for...

ribcage

LEARN THE BODY PARTS WITH THE ALPHABET

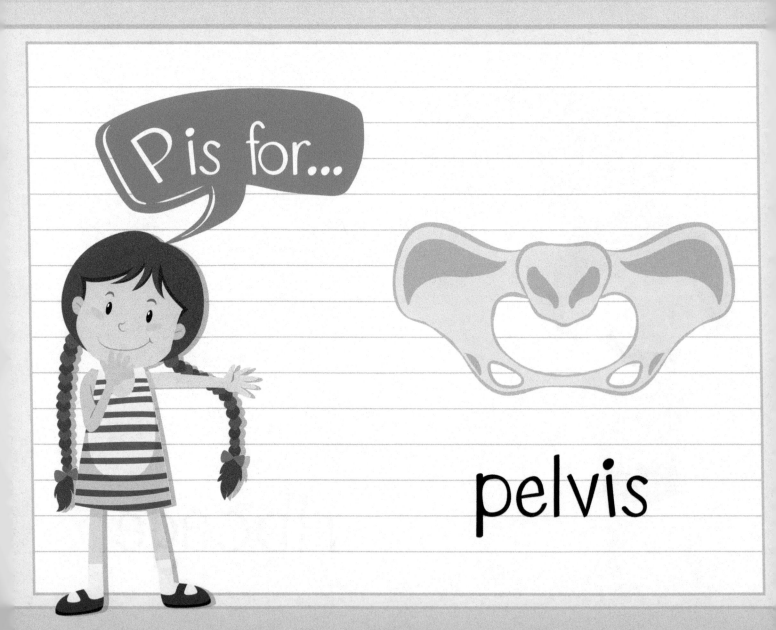

LEARN THE BODY PARTS WITH THE ALPHABET

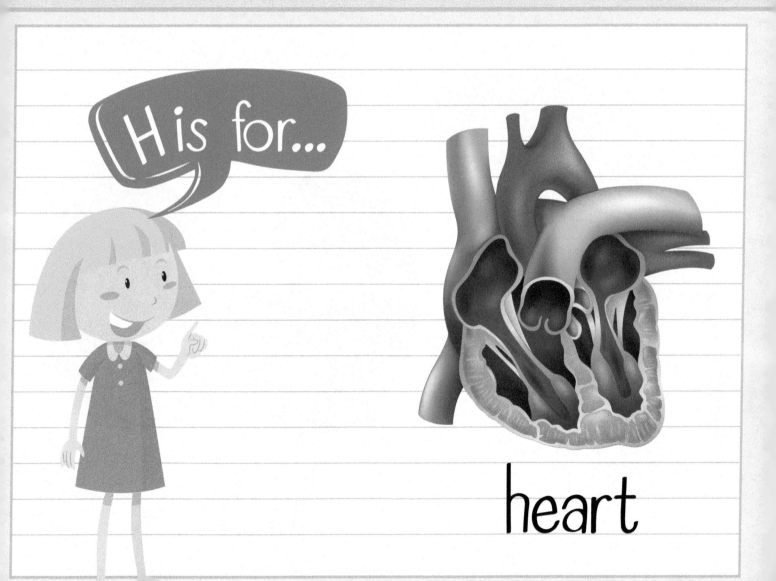

LEARN THE BODY PARTS WITH THE ALPHABET

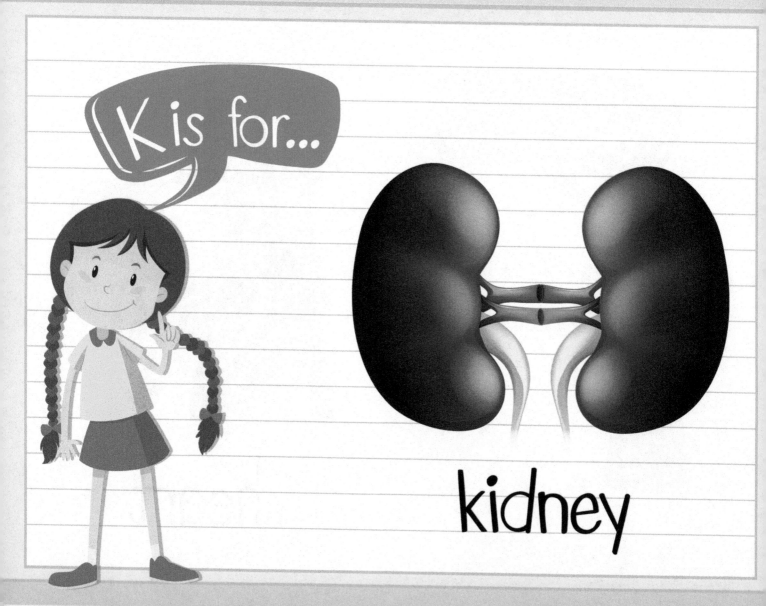

LEARN THE BODY PARTS WITH THE ALPHABET

THE BODY

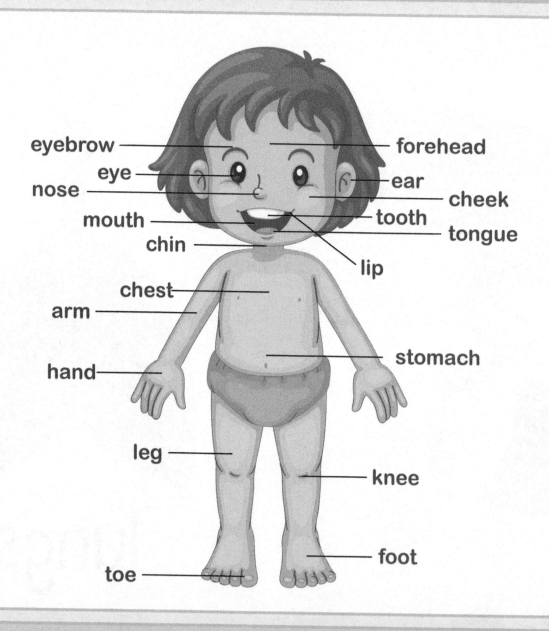

eyebrow —
eye —
nose —
mouth —
chin —
forehead
ear
cheek
tooth
tongue
lip
chest
arm
hand
stomach
leg
knee
foot
toe

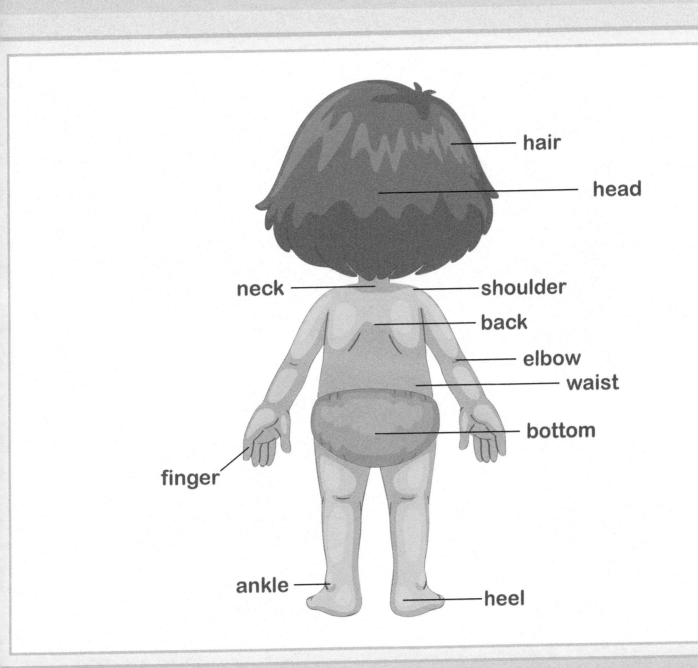

hair

head

neck — shoulder

back

elbow

waist

bottom

finger

ankle

heel

THE EYE

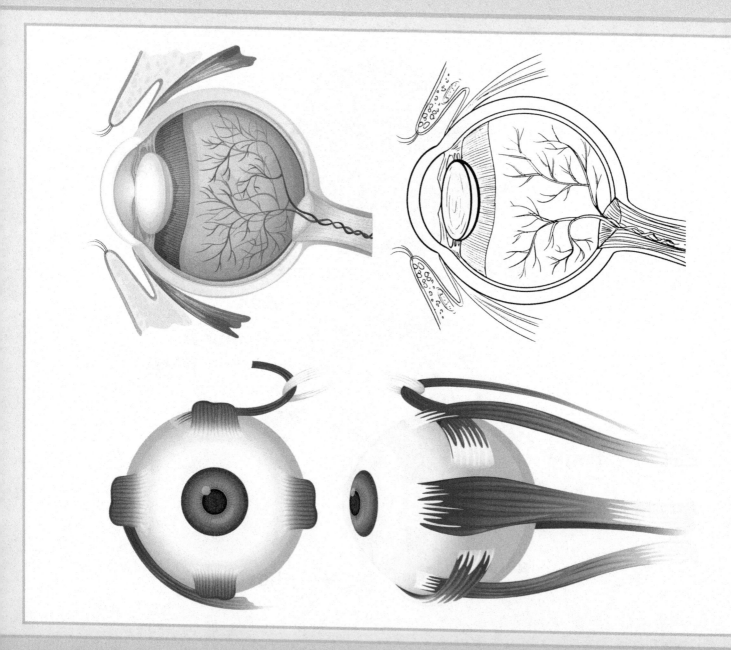

MUSCLES OF THE EYE

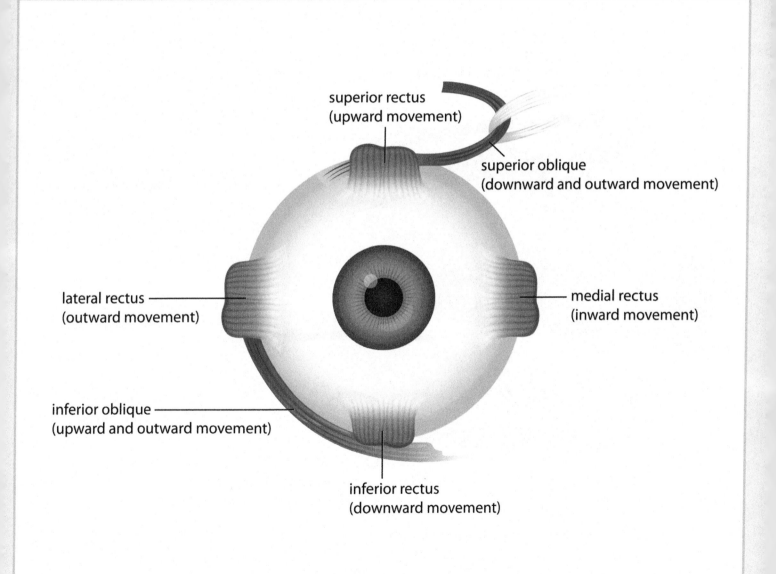

superior rectus
(upward movement)

superior oblique
(downward and outward movement)

lateral rectus
(outward movement)

medial rectus
(inward movement)

inferior oblique
(upward and outward movement)

inferior rectus
(downward movement)

MUSCLES OF THE EYE

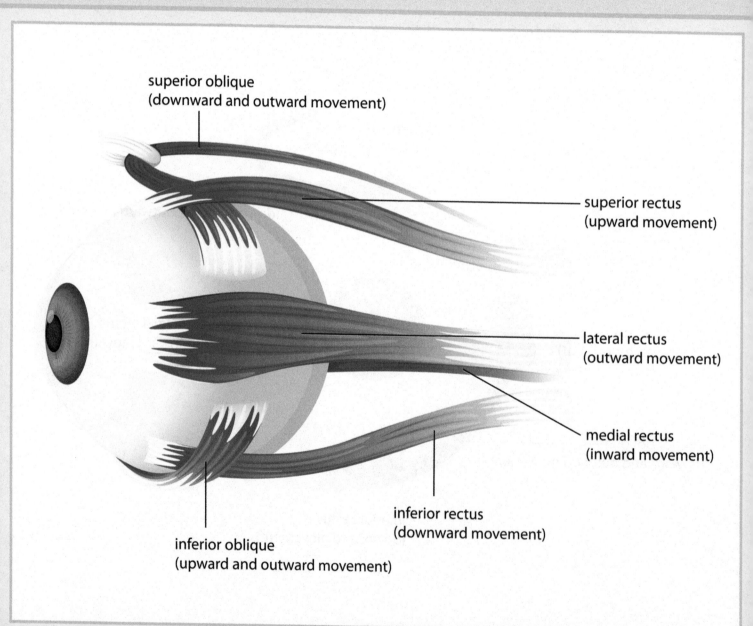

superior oblique
(downward and outward movement)

superior rectus
(upward movement)

lateral rectus
(outward movement)

medial rectus
(inward movement)

inferior rectus
(downward movement)

inferior oblique
(upward and outward movement)

ANATOMY OF THE EYE

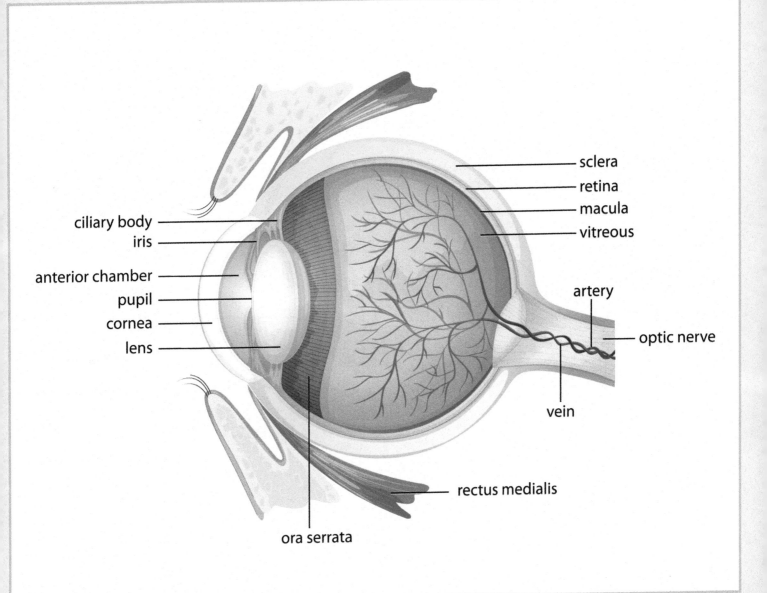

ciliary body

iris

anterior chamber

pupil

cornea

lens

sclera

retina

macula

vitreous

artery

optic nerve

vein

rectus medialis

ora serrata

THE NOSE

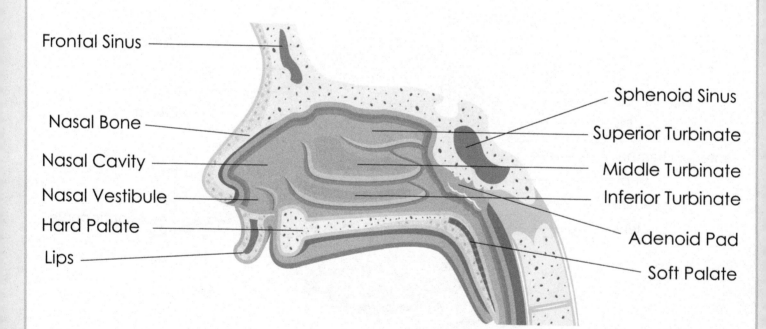

Frontal Sinus

Nasal Bone

Nasal Cavity

Nasal Vestibule

Hard Palate

Lips

Sphenoid Sinus

Superior Turbinate

Middle Turbinate

Inferior Turbinate

Adenoid Pad

Soft Palate

THE EAR

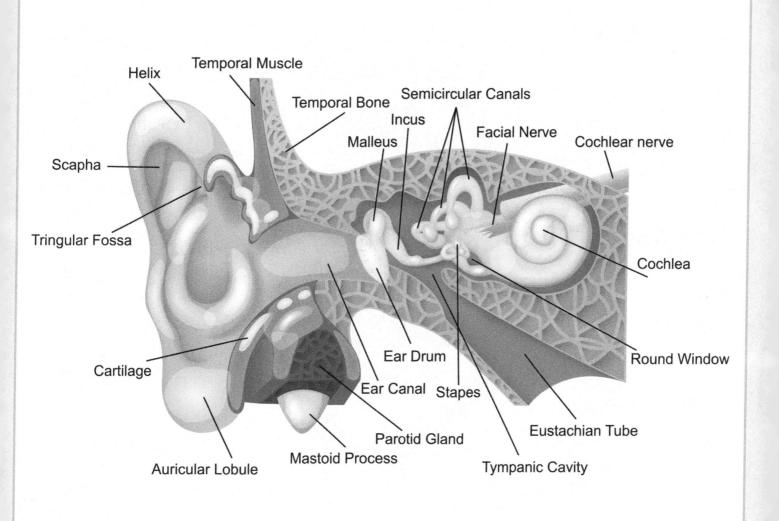

THE MOUTH

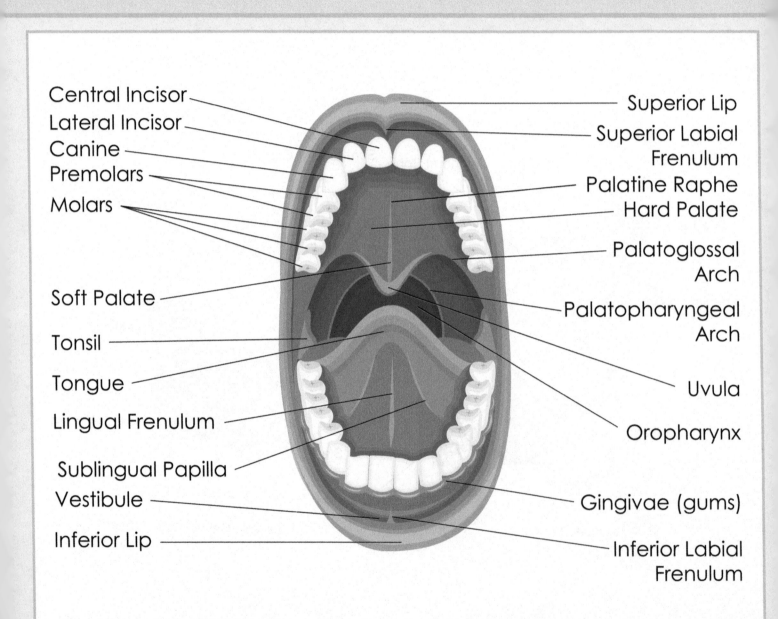

Central Incisor

Lateral Incisor

Canine

Premolars

Molars

Soft Palate

Tonsil

Tongue

Lingual Frenulum

Sublingual Papilla

Vestibule

Inferior Lip

Superior Lip

Superior Labial Frenulum

Palatine Raphe

Hard Palate

Palatoglossal Arch

Palatopharyngeal Arch

Uvula

Oropharynx

Gingivae (gums)

Inferior Labial Frenulum

THE TONGUE

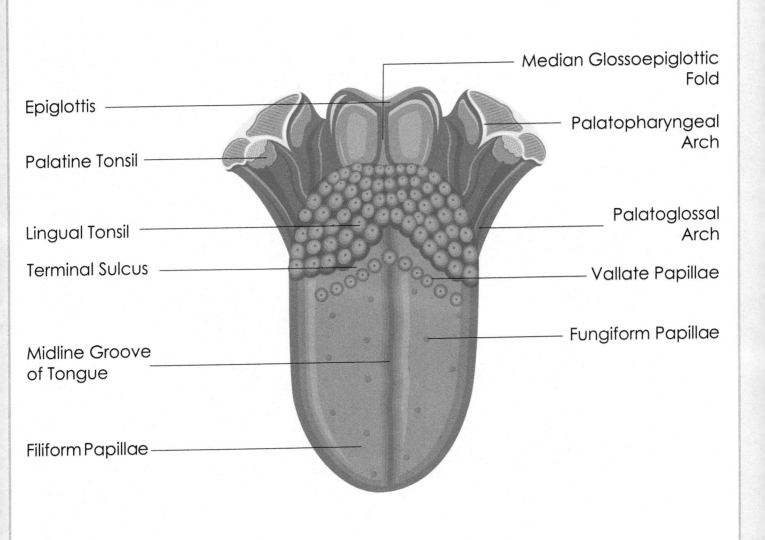

Median Glossoepiglottic Fold

Epiglottis

Palatopharyngeal Arch

Palatine Tonsil

Lingual Tonsil

Palatoglossal Arch

Terminal Sulcus

Vallate Papillae

Fungiform Papillae

Midline Groove of Tongue

Filiform Papillae

THE TOOTH

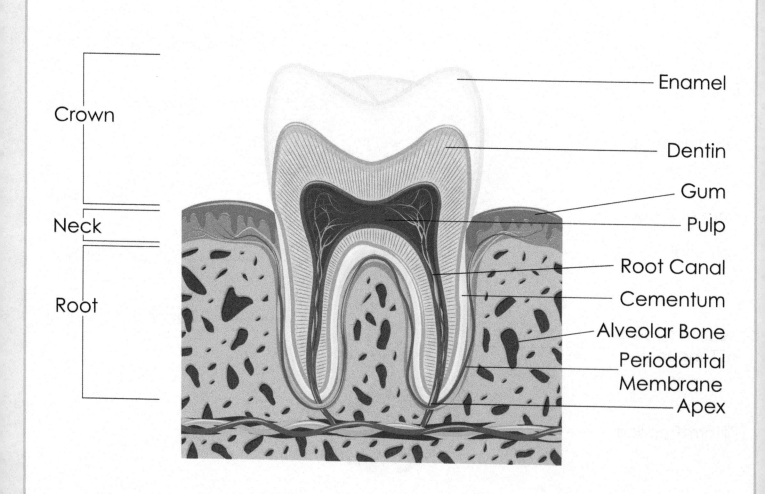

Crown

Neck

Root

Enamel

Dentin

Gum

Pulp

Root Canal

Cementum

Alveolar Bone

Periodontal Membrane

Apex

HUMAN SKIN & HAIR

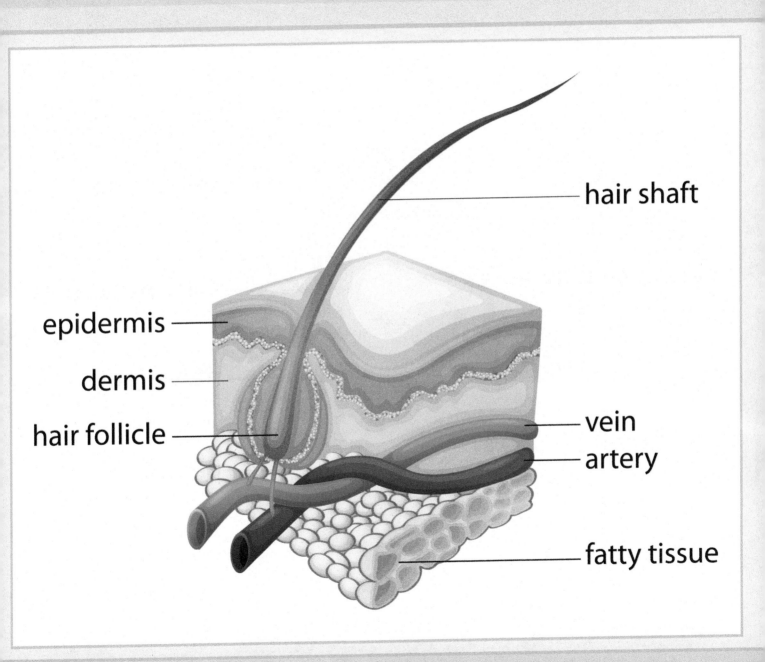

hair shaft

epidermis

dermis

hair follicle

vein

artery

fatty tissue

HUMAN VERTEBRAE

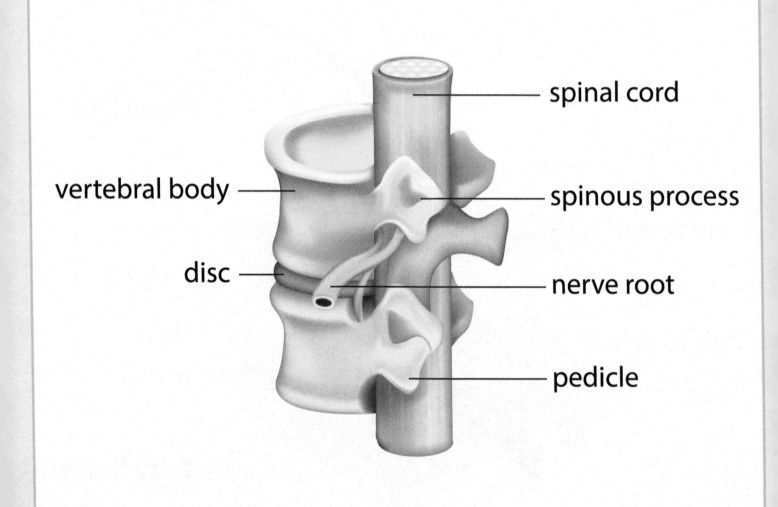

spinal cord

vertebral body

spinous process

disc

nerve root

pedicle

Let's practice what we have learned so far by labeling some diagrams

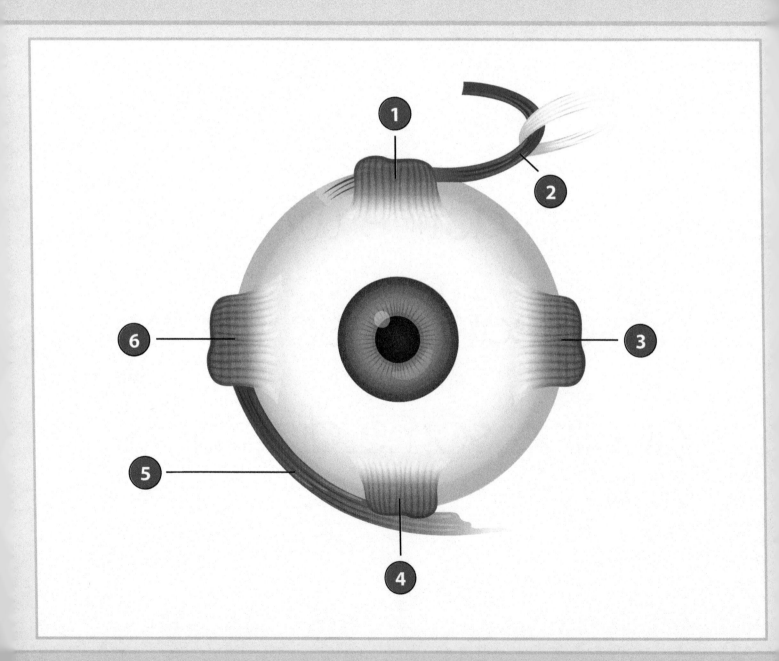

LIST THE PARTS NUMBERED

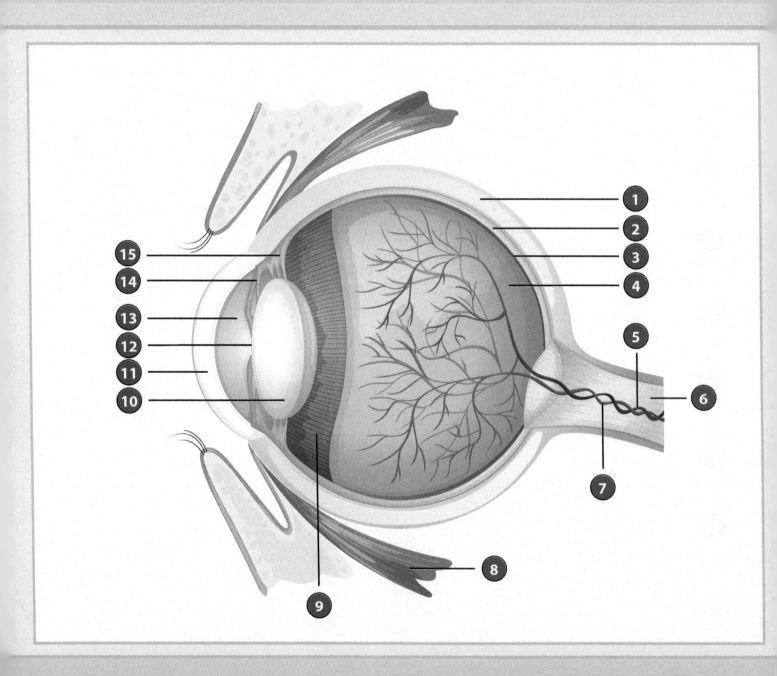

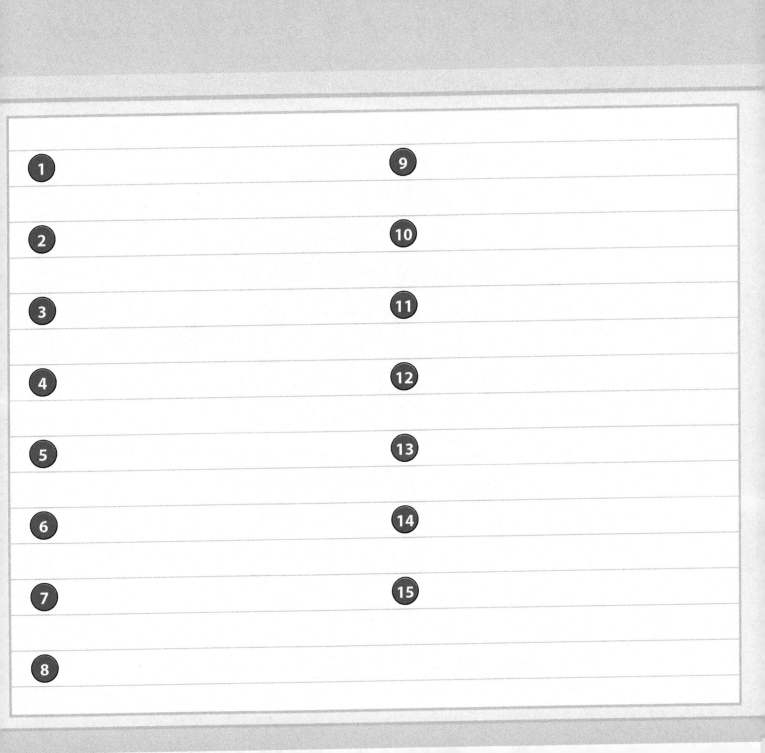

LIST THE PARTS NUMBERED

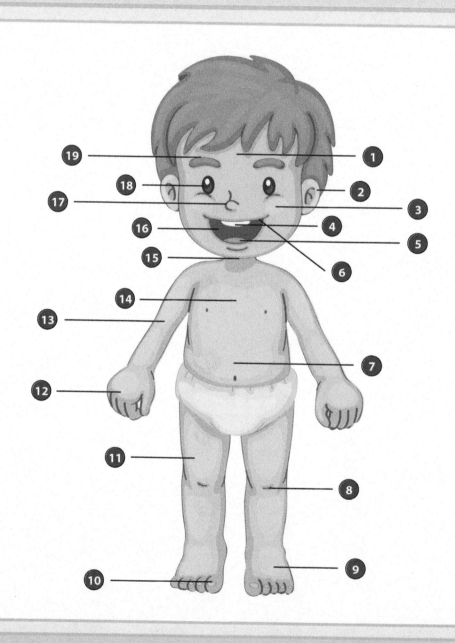

LIST THE PARTS NUMBERED

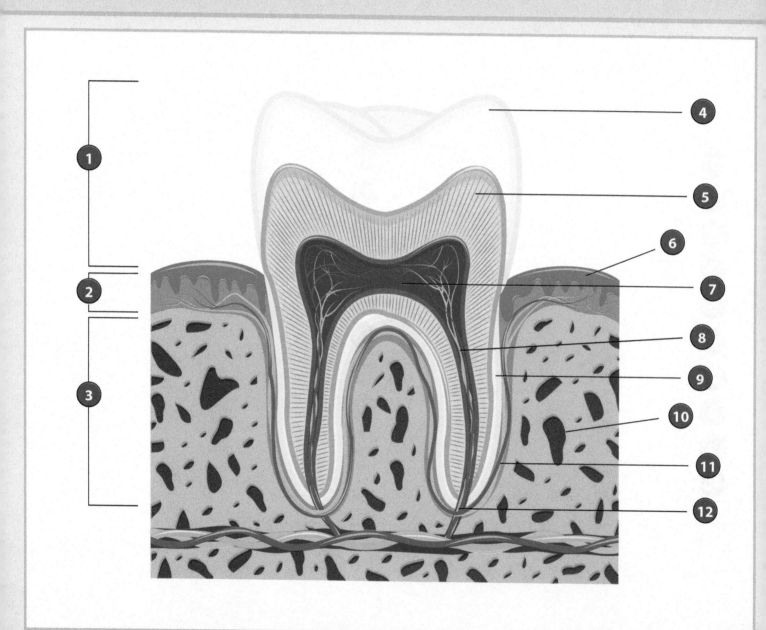

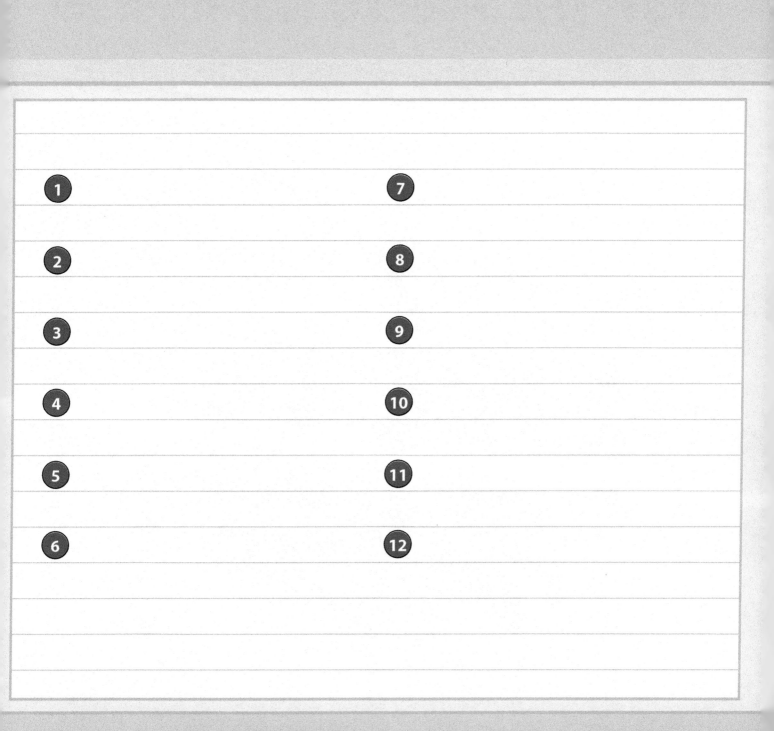

LIST THE PARTS NUMBERED

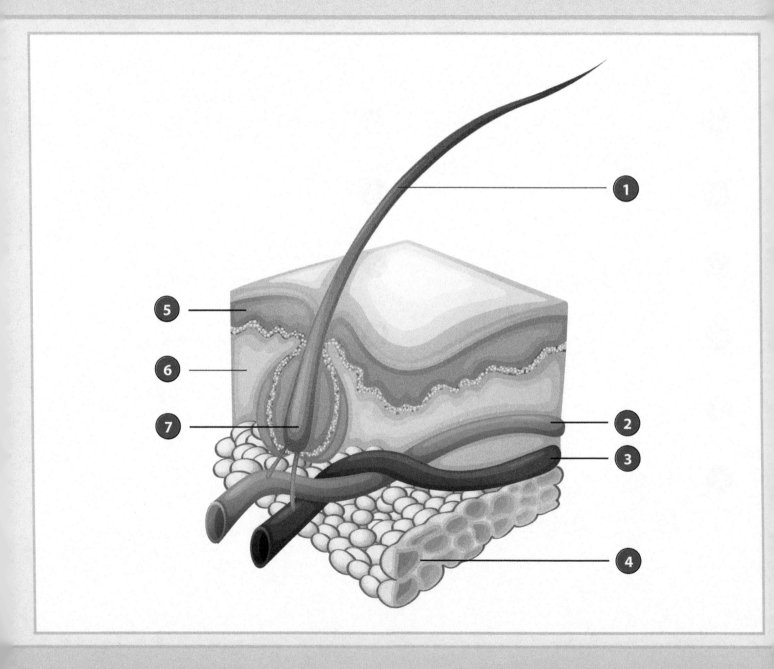

ANSWERS

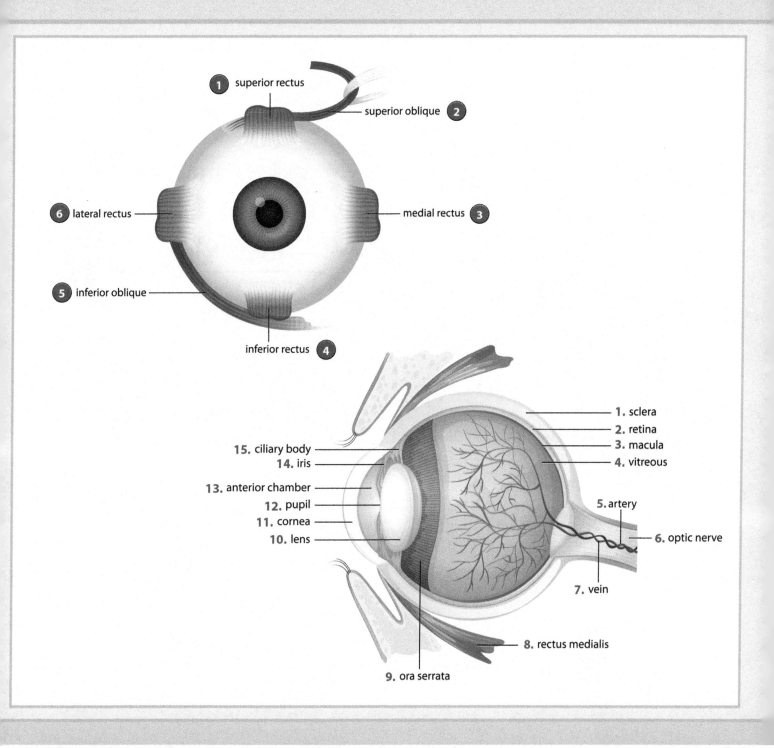

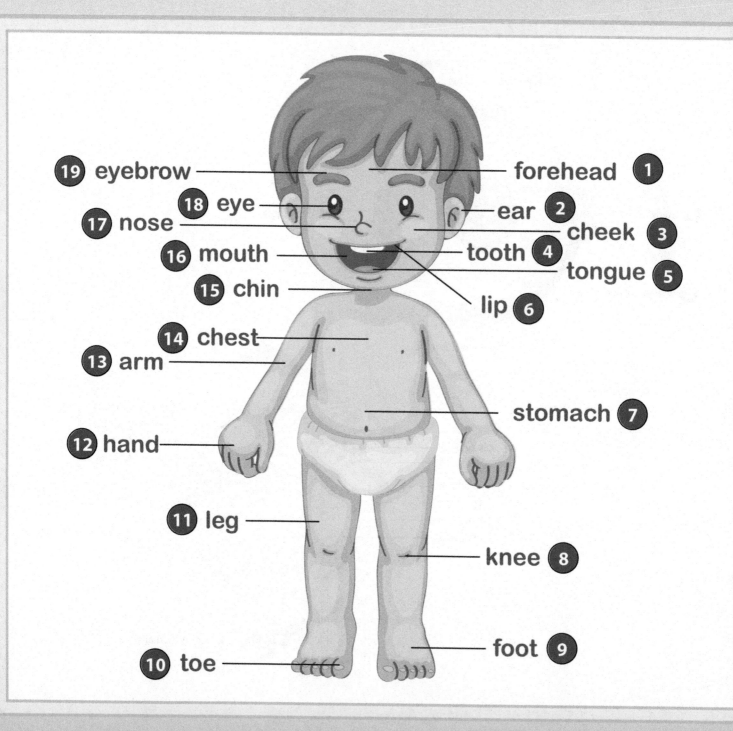

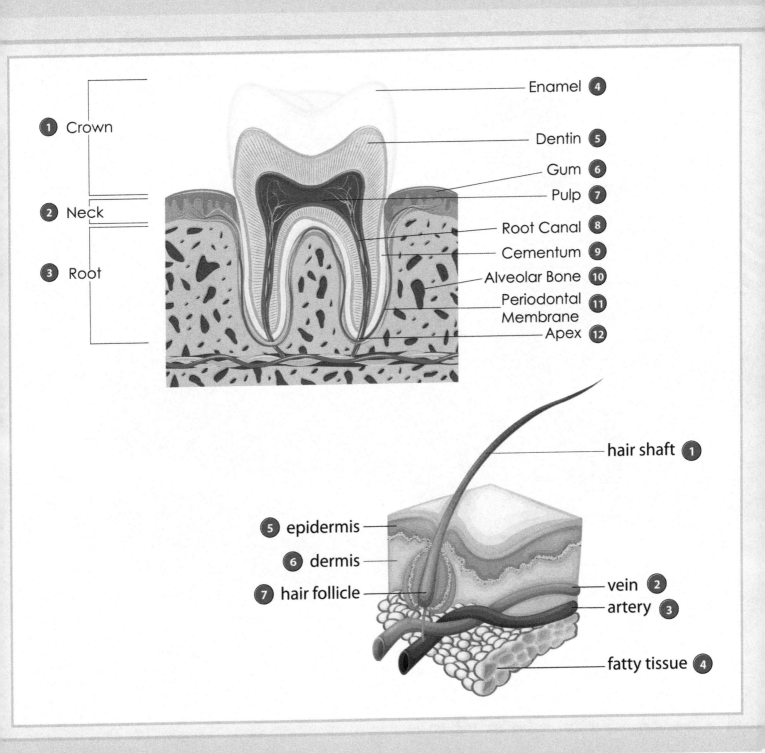

1 Crown

2 Neck

3 Root

Enamel 4

Dentin 5

Gum 6

Pulp 7

Root Canal 8

Cementum 9

Alveolar Bone 10

Periodontal 11
Membrane

Apex 12

hair shaft 1

5 epidermis

6 dermis

7 hair follicle

vein 2

artery 3

fatty tissue 4

Visit

BABY PROFESSOR
EDUCATION KIDS

www.BabyProfessorBooks.com

to download Free Baby Professor eBooks
and view our catalog of new and exciting
Children's Books

CPSIA information can be obtained
at www.ICGtesting.com
Printed in the USA
LVOW05s0443020118
561465LV00007B/212/P

9 781541 940383